Rolling in the Aisles

Cal and Rose Samra

WATERBROOK
PRESS

ROLLING IN THE AISLES
PUBLISHED BY WATERBROOK PRESS
5446 North Academy Boulevard, Suite 200
Colorado Springs, Colorado 80918
A division of Random House, Inc.

For information about the Fellowship of Merry Christians and *The Joyful Noiseletter,*
please call toll-free 1-800-877-2757 from 8 A.M. to 5 P.M. E.S.T. M-F or write:
FMC, PO Box 895, Portage, MI 49081-0895. E-mail: JoyfulNZ@aol.com Visit
FMC's website: www.JoyfulNoiseletter.com

Library of Congress Cataloging-in-Publication Data
Rolling in the aisles / [compiled] by Cal and Rose Samra
      p.   cm.
   ISBN 1-57856-285-6
   1. Christian life Humor. 2. Christianity Humor. 3. Church Humor.
I. Samra, Cal. II. Samra, Rose.
PN6231.C35R65   1999
230'.002'07—dc21   99-33693
                                                    CIP

Printed in the United States of America
1999—First Edition

10 9 8 7 6 5 4 3 2 1

*Laughter is the sun that drives winter
from the human face.*

—Victor Hugo

PREFACE

"Humor," wrote theologian Reinhold Niebuhr, "is the prelude to faith, and laughter is the beginning of prayer."

The words "humor" and "humility" have the same Latin roots. Humor teaches us humility. Humor shows us how far each of us has fallen short of the glory of God.

Ironically, holy humor both humbles us and lifts our spirits. It is one of the many gifts of God.

Here are some gifts of laughter from the Fellowship of Merry Christians.

—CAL AND ROSE SAMRA
EDITORS, *THE JOYFUL NOISELETTER*

THE BEST OF THE CHURCH BULLETIN BLOOPERS

Bloopers and typos have bedeviled church bulletins, as well as other publications, for centuries. Here are some of our favorite bloopers, passed on to The Joyful Noiseletter *by churches and persons of all denominations.*

At a wedding attended by FMC member Marvin Breshears of Yakima, Washington, the processional hymn for the seating of the mothers was printed in the wedding bulletin as "Come Undo Me" instead of "Come Unto Me."

From the bulletin of a Phoenix Baptist church: "Children's choir will now be hell on Sunday nights."

—VIA REV. DENNIS DANIEL, FOUNTAIN HILLS, ARIZONA

Classified ad in the *Nickel Ads* in Wenatchee, Washington: "Newer wood church pews, sleeps six, $100 each."

—VIA LES FOLTZ, JR., BELLEVUE, WASHINGTON

From Sherrill, Iowa: "10:30 A.M. worship Communion candle lighting in remembrance of those who have died during the last year at both worship services."

—VIA SR. MARY OWEN HAGGERTY, SINSINAWA, WISCONSIN

Blooper in the April 12, 1998, *Crystal Cathedral Sunday*, the bulletin of the Crystal Cathedral in Garden Grove, California:

"Remember in Prayer:

"Matilda_____, awaiting surgery to remove large brain behind the eye."

—VIA DR. JACK W. TALLMAN, TUSTIN, CALIFORNIA

In the bulletin of Peace Lutheran Church, Smyrna, Delaware:

"Pray for our church and Pastor and Mrs. Krompart as we consider their proposal to help us here at Peace. Let's not sit back and take them for granite, but receive, welcome, and work with them."

—VIA REV. JAMES A. LANGE, LEWES, DELAWARE

Blooper in a Catholic church bulletin: "The church had a going-away party for Father _____. The congregation was anxious to give him a little momentum."

—VIA JOSEPH A. MAHER, OXNARD, CALIFORNI

From a church bulletin: "Eight new choir robes are needed due to the addition of several new members and the deterioration of some older ones."

—VIA GEORGE GOLDTRAP, ORMOND-BY-THE-SEA, FLORIDA

"If it please the court, my client would like to withdraw that last remark about letting him who is without sin cast the first stone."

© Ed Sullivan

In the bulletin of St. Elizabeth Ann Seton Catholic Church, Palm Coast, Florida:

"We will have a Special Holiday Bingo & Dinner on Monday evening, December 30. You will be given two Bingo packs, which cover all games played, and your choice of children or roast beef for dinner."

—VIA REV. FREDERICK R. PARKE

The closing worship chorus at Ames United Methodist Church in Saginaw, Michigan, was the majestic "The Dwelling of God Is Among You Today." But the worshipers doubled over with laughter when they read the lines in the church bulletin:

"And then I heard a loud voice say,
'Behold, the dwelling of God is among you today!
'And He shall wipe away your rears...'"

—LAWRENCE BROOKS, SAGINAW, MICHIGAN

From the newsletter of St. Matthews Lutheran Church, St. Paul, Minnesota:

"Adult Forum. Beginning November 5, Pastor Hodges will lead a six-part series on the book of Genesis. Were Adam and Eve really naked in the garden? Come and see for yourself."

—PALMER RUSCHKE, ST. PAUL, MINNESOTA

From a church bulletin: "The audience is asked to remain seated until the end of the recession."

—VIA PATTY WOOTEN, SANTA CRUZ, CALIFORNIA

From Australia came this church bulletin blooper, passed on by Dr. Geoff Pankhurst, pastor of the Uniting Church in Orange, Australia:

"Thursday night—Potluck Supper. Prayer and medication to follow."

"Well, if you don't believe in the organized church, you'll love ours—we're as disorganized as they come!"

Blooper in a Catholic church bulletin: "Father _____ has spoken in the largest Catholic churches in America. To miss hearing him will be the chance of a lifetime."

—VIA JOSEPH A. MAHER, OXNARD, CALIFORNIA

Rev. Grace T. Lawrence, pastor of the First Baptist Church of Lykens, Pennsylvania, writes that the church's "Good News Letter" carried the following report on the prayer group meeting:

"On March 16th, the prayer group met at the home of _____, who is no longer able to attend church. What a blessing!"

⑥

Blooper in a church Christmas bulletin: "The choir will sing 'I Heard the Bills on Christmas Day.'"

From a church bulletin: "Low Self-Esteem Support Group will meet at 8 P.M. Wednesday. Please use the back door."

—VIA PATTY WOOTEN, RN, SANTA CRUZ, CALIFORNIA

In the bulletin of St. Lawrence the Martyr Parish Community of Chester, New Jersey: "There will be blessing of expectant parents on Sunday after all Masses. All expectant parents please go to the front pews and wail for the priest."

From the bulletin of St. Francis of Assisi Church in Bradford, Pennsylvania: "Father John _____ will be the homeliest each evening."

—VIA WILLIAM J. O'DONNELL

From the church bulletin of St. Francis de Sales Church, Albany, New York: "Wednesday, May 9, is Ascension Thursday."

—VIA KATHLEEN SHEA, HAWORTH, NEW JERSEY

The church bulletin of Westminster Presbyterian Church in Portland, Oregon, carried the following note from Mrs. Roma Church, age eighty, who had been hospitalized: "Thank you so very much, my dead friends, for the lovely cards, phone calls, and visits during my recent accident and subsequent recovery. Hope to be with you soon. Lovingly, Roma."

—VIA BUD FRIMOTH, PORTLAND, OREGON

From the bulletin of Peace Lutheran Church, Manhattan, Kansas: "Before the lecture he will be discussing his personal faith struggle in suffering at a potluck supper."

From a Magnolia, North Carolina, church bulletin: "If you choose to heave during the postlude, please do so quietly so as not to interrupt those remaining for worship and meditation."

—VIA REV. PAUL J. DAVIS, SCOTTSDALE, ARIZONA

Classified ad under employment opportunities in a Los Angeles newspaper:

"Position requires: wisdom of Solomon, patience of Job, skill of David. No other applicants have a prayer."

Classified ad in *The Criterion*, Catholic archdiocesan newspaper of Indianapolis: "Christian live-in female companion needed by older lady. Must have ear."

—VIA JOSEPH L. HENLEY, BEDFORD, INDIANA

"We can remember George as a convicted counterfeiter or as an unselfish and generous individual who paid off the church deficit."

Dr. Alan C. Rhodes of Grace United Methodist Church, Ravena, New York, spotted this blooper in his hometown newspaper, *The Press-Republican* of Plattsburgh, New York:

"_____ is consecrated today as the eighth bishop of the Episcopal Diocese of Albany at the New York State Convention Center. The Presiding Bishop of the Episcopal Church of the United States leads other bishops, parish priests, deacons, and laity in the festive occasion. It continues the church's tradition of an unbroken line of apostasy dating back to the original twelve apostles."

From the *Dalton (Georgia) Daily Citizen News*:

"John _____, ordained as a deamon, will pastor two churches in Fannin County."

—VIA REV. DUSTIN PENNINGTON
FIRST ASSEMBLY OF GOD, DALTON, GEORGIA

From a minister's letter published in a farm magazine: "I have pestered rural churches for nearly thirty years."

—VIA REV. DENNY BRAKE, RALEIGH, NORTH CAROLINA

Rev. Henry E. Riley, Jr., of Chesterfield, Virginia, passed on this story from the last century when typesetters used movable hot-type. The typesetter of an English newspaper mixed up the lead slugs on two news stories—one reporting on a new pig-killing, sausage-making machine and the other reporting on a pastor's retirement party. Here's how the story appeared in the newspaper:

"Several of the Rev. Dr. Mudge's friends called upon him yesterday, and after a conversation, the unsuspecting pig was seized by the hind leg and slid along a beam until he reached the hot water tank…

"Thereupon he came forward and said that there were times when the feelings overpowered one, and for that reason, he would not attempt to do more than thank those around him for the manner in which such a huge animal was cut into fragments was simply astonishing.

"The doctor concluded his remarks, when the machine seized him, and in less time than it takes to write it, the pig was cut into fragments and worked up into delicious sausage. The occasion will be long remembered by the doctor's friends as one of the most delightful of their lives. The best pieces can be procured for tenpence a pound, and we are sure that those who have sat so long under his ministry will rejoice that he has been treated so handsomely."

In a church bulletin: "For those of you who have children and don't know it, we have a nursery downstairs."

"Meet Howard Meely… perpetual sermon illustration."

© Bill Frauhiger

Headline in *Centre View*, a northern Virginia newspaper: "Holy Spirit Now Officially Lutheran." The article below it was about the organization of a new church, Holy Spirit Lutheran Church in Centreville, Virginia.

Following a lengthy and heated congregational meeting, the secretary presented the minutes for the pastor's review. The pastor reviewed them and asked the secretary to read her report of the motion to establish an executive committee. Her record of the motion stated, "We need to establish an execution committee."

—REV. GERALD R. O'CONNOR
IMMANUEL UNITED CHURCH OF CHRIST,
BARTLETT, ILLINOIS

In his syndicated column in the *Arizona Republic,* evange-list Billy Graham advised a young virgin in high school to remain celibate: "The Bible is clear: 'Flee from sexual immortality.'"

—VIA GINA BRIDGEMAN, SCOTTSDALE, ARIZONA

From the *Fort Scott* (Kansas) *Tribune:* "The winners of the 1997 Light Up Fort Scott Christmas lighting contest (spon-sored by the Kiwanis Pioneers) have been announced. Signs will be placed in the sinners' yards during the Christmas season to recognize their efforts."

—VIA REV. ROBERT H. LAPP
FIRST PRESBYTERIAN CHURCH, FORT SCOTT, KANSAS

Headline in ad of Unity Church on the church page of the *News Press* in Fort Myers, Florida: "Come Grown with Us."

—VIA CARL E. WAGNER, JR., TOWSON, MARYLAND

© Dik LaPine

Typo in a circular letter to priests in Philadelphia from Rev. Hans A. L. Brouwers, archdiocesan director, concerning preparations for World Mission Sunday:

"You will soon receive, as part of the September archdiocesan Priest's Monthly Mailing, a Liturgy Guide, and a Massage from His Holiness Pope John Paul II for World Mission Sunday."

In the call to worship printed in the bulletin of First Presbyterian Church of Shadyside, Ohio, after the congregation read the line "God has not forgotten us," the lay liturgist was supposed to read the line "Could a mother forget the child she has nurtured?" Instead, the liturgist read, "Could a mother forget the child she has neutered?"

—REV. ALICE L. PHILLIPS

From the yearbook of Trinity Lutheran Church, Jeffers, Minnesota:

"The [correspondence] committee will assist with the mailing of the newsletter and stapling of the Annual Report to congregational members."

The annual report of the female president to the congregation of First English Lutheran Church, Kimball, Nebraska, declared:

"We as a congregation have achieved many accomplishments. We have been truly blessed in our missions and ministry. All of the broads have done an excellent job."

—MRS. DWAYNE HUNZEKER, KIMBALL, NEBRASKA

A cake decorator in New Zealand was asked to inscribe 1 John 4:18—"There is no fear in love, but perfect love casteth out fear"—on a wedding cake. The decorator misread the reference, and when the cake arrived at the wedding reception, it was discovered that John 4:18 was inscribed on the cake:

> *"For thou hast had*
> *five husbands, and he whom*
> *thou now hast is not*
> *thy husband."*

—VIA HAROLD W. BRETZ, INDIANAPOLIS, INDIANA

In the bulletin of the Westchester (Illinois) Community United Church of Christ:

"And we give You thanks, O God, for people of many cultures and nations; for the young and old and muddle-aged."

The caption beneath a photograph of the St. Olaf College choir in the *Sun Cities* (Arizona) *Independent* described the choir as "internationally renounced."

During the dark days of World War II, a devout Frenchman in the underground telegraphed this message to supporters in England:

"God reigns!" But the message was garbled in transit and came out "God resigns!" The English wired back: "Regret decision. British policy remains the same."

—VIA *THE ANGLICAN DIGEST*

"The joy of the LORD is your strength."
—NEHEMIAH 8:10 (NASB)

The Assembly of God Church of Bushnell, Florida, received a computerized sweepstakes notice announcing that "God, of Bushnell, Florida" was a finalist for the eleven-million-dollar top prize.

"God, we've been searching for you," the letter from American Family Publishers said. "If you win, what an incredible fortune there would be for God! Could you imagine the looks you'd get from your neighbors? But don't just sit there, God."

Commented Pastor Bill Brack: "I always thought He lived here, but I didn't actually know. Now I do. He's got a P.O. box here."

When a bit of sunshine hits ye,
After passing of a cloud,
When a fit of laughter gits ye,
An' yer spine is feelin' proud,
Don't fergit to up and fling it
At a soul that's feelin' blue,
For the minute that ye sling it,
It's a boomerang to you!
— *John Wallace Crawford*
American poet and frontier scout (1847)

—VIA PASTOR JOHN J. WALKER

A church bulletin announced the coffee hour: "Thirst after Righteousness."

—DICK FRIEDLINE
FIRST CHRISTIAN CHURCH, VENTURA, CALIFORNIA

SPOONERISMS

An Anglican clergyman, the Rev. William Archibald Spooner (1844–1930) is regarded as the all-time champion of the verbal blooper. Spooner, the warden of New College in Oxford, England, gave his name to a form of crazy talk known as "spoonerisms."

A spoonerism is an unintentional transposition of sounds in two or more words. For instance, Rev. Spooner once told a rector: "The vicar knows every crook and nanny in the parish."

One Sunday morning, Spooner told his congregation: "Let us sing 'The Kinkering Congs Their Tattles Tike.'" The hymn was "The Conquering Kings Their Titles Take."

On another occasion, he announced the next hymn would be "From Iceland's Greasy Mountains." At a wedding, he told the groom, "It is kistomary to cuss the bride."

In those days, pews were rented by members of Spooner's Anglican congregation. One Sunday morning, Spooner told a woman: "Madam, you are occupewing the wrong pie. Let me sew you to your sheet."

Spooner, who taught history at Oxford, England, once said to a nonproductive student: "You have hissed all your mystery lectures and have completely tasted two whole worms."

Spooner once preached sympathetically about a man who "had received a blushing crow." He meant to say "crushing blow."

Another time he preached about "the tearful chidings of the Gospel." He meant "cheerful tidings."

He once observed that, "although people differ in rank and station, at death they are all brought to a red devil." He meant to say "dead level."

Calling on the dean of Christ Church, he asked the secretary, "Is the bean dizzy?" Giving the eulogy at a clergyman's funeral, he praised his departed colleague as a "shoving leopard to his flock."

In another sermon, he warned his congregation: "There is no peace in a home where a dinner swells." He intended to say "where a sinner dwells."

Speaking to a group of farmers, Spooner intended to greet them as "sons of toil," but said, "I see before me tons of soil."

"The head thinks, the hands labor,
but it's the heart that laughs!."
—LIZ CURTIS HIGGS

"Have you ever noticed that whenever the pastor leaves on vacation, he always gets a replacement who talks longer than he would?"

DAFFYNITIONS

Preacher: a person who talks in someone else's sleep.
Ministerial pride: altar ego.

—FRED SEVIER, SUN CITY, ARIZONA

Atheism: a non-prophet organization.

—VIA REV. KARL R. KRAFT, MANTUA, NEW JERSEY

Atheist: a person with no invisible means of support.

—OSCAR LEVANT

Deacongestion: too many deacons at a meeting.

—LOWELL J. GOERING, HILLSBORO, KANSAS

© Goddard Sherman

Mark Twain once attended a church service where a missionary appealed for funds to evangelize the heathen in a foreign land. "After ten minutes of a description about their unhappy plight, I wanted to give fifty dollars," Twain wrote. "The preacher kept on another fifteen minutes and that gave me time to realize that fifty dollars was an extravagance, so I cut it in half. At the end of another ten minutes, I had reduced it to five dollars. When at the end of an hour of speaking the plates were finally passed, I was so annoyed that I reached in and helped myself to a quarter."

"Walk a mile in his shoes before you criticize a man. Then, if he gets angry, you're a mile away and he's barefoot."

—AUTHOR UNKNOWN

Taken from a young student's examination paper: "A virtuoso is a musician with real high morals."

—Sr. Mary Laurentina Taffee, Farmington Hills, Michigan

Campaigning through his state, the late Sen. Clyde Hoey of North Carolina stopped at a church in a small town and was greeted by the minister. "How many members do you have in your church?" the senator asked.

"Fifty," the pastor replied.

"And how many active members?"

"Fifty."

"Fifty members and fifty active? You must be a good preacher!" the senator said.

"Yes, sir—fifty members," the minister said. "Twenty-five active for me and twenty-five active against me."

—William C. S. Pellowe, *Laughter under the Steeple*

"Punch in with me, if you will, 1 Corinthians, thirteenth chapter . . ."

© Steve Phelps

*Evelyn Briscoe of Okmulgee, Oklahoma, went to the First Pres-
byterian Church in Sapulpa, Oklahoma, to hear author Charlie
Shedd preach. Mrs. Briscoe heard Shedd tell this story:*

A college drama group presented a play in which one
character would stand on a trapdoor and announce, "I
descend into hell!" A stagehand below would then pull a
rope, the trapdoor would open, and the character would
plunge through. The play was well received.

When the actor playing the part became ill, another
actor who was quite overweight took his place. When the
new actor announced, "I descend into hell!" the stagehand pulled the rope, and the actor began his plunge, but
became hopelessly stuck. No amount of tugging on the
rope could make him descend.

One student in the balcony jumped up and yelled:
"Hallelujah! Hell is full!"

"After a worship service at First Baptist Church in New Castle, Kentucky, a mother with a fidgety seven-year-old boy told me how she finally got her son to sit still and be quiet. About halfway through the sermon, she leaned over and whispered: 'If you don't be quiet, Pastor Charlton is going to lose his place and will have to start his sermon all over again!' It worked."

—PASTOR DAVE CHARLTON, NEW CASTLE, KENTUCKY

I go to sleep
By counting sheep.
I preach—to sheep
I put to sleep.

—MSGR. ARTHUR TONNE, *JOKES PRIESTS CAN TELL*

"Try to give more than your
usual dollar, Harry."

The *Tennessean* of Nashville sponsored a limerick contest.
One of the winners was submitted by Georgia Byers:

> Our preacher, the Reverend Grundy,
> > Baptized my sister last Sunday;
> But he lost his grip
> > And she turned to flip—
> She's expected to surface next Monday.

Bob Horner, a postal worker, submitted this limerick
about Baby Boomers:

> As Boomers, we once loudly vented
> > On evils that should be repented.
> But as years have gone by,
> > We cannot deny
> We became all the things we lamented.

—VIA GEORGE GOLDTRAP, ORMOND-BY-THE-SEA, FLORIDA

When a new building had to be constructed on Vatican grounds, the architect submitted the plans to Pope John XXIII, who shortly afterward returned them with these three Latin words written in the margin: *Non sumus angeli*, meaning, "We are not angels." The architect and his staff couldn't figure out what the Pope meant until finally someone noticed that the plans did not include bathrooms.

—MSGR. ARTHUR TONNE, *JOKES PRIESTS CAN TELL*

"I would rather try and cool down a fanatic than try and warm up a corpse."

—JOHN WESLEY

"Some ministers would make good martyrs; they are so dry they would burn well."

—CHARLES HADDON SPURGEON

A Catholic man has a heart attack and falls on a sidewalk of a city street. "Get me a priest!" the dying man tells a police officer coming to his aid.

The police officer asks the gathering crowd if there is a priest among them. No one comes forward.

"I need a priest, please!" the dying man cries out.

Finally, an elderly man in the crowd steps forward and says, "Officer, I'm not a priest or a Catholic, but for many years I lived next to a Catholic church, and every night I listened to the Catholic litany. Maybe I can be of some comfort to this poor man."

The old man kneels down next to the dying man and says solemnly: "O-72, G-51, B-5, N-33, I-20…"

—VIA BUD FRIMOTH, PORTLAND, OREGON

Eager to improve his sermons, a young pastor bought a tape recorder and recorded one of his Sunday morning services. After dinner, he put the cassette in the recorder, sat on the sofa, and listened to the tape.

The opening prayer, Scripture readings, and hymns came forth nicely. Then came the sermon.

When he awoke some time later, the choir was singing the closing hymn.

—MSGR. ARTHUR TONNE, *JOKES PRIESTS CAN TELL*

Rev. Steve W. Caraway, pastor of University United Methodist Church, Lake Charles, Louisiana, told his congregation: "I have good news and bad news about our pledges. The good news is: we have reached our goal. The bad news is: you still have them in your pocket."

—VIA EDWARD MORRIS, WEST ISLIP, NEW YORK

TOP TEN PICK-UP LINES AT A SINGLES' CHURCH

10. "Hi. This pew taken?"

9. "My prayers are answered."

8. "What's a charismatic like you doing in a main-line place like this?"

7. "How about we go over to my place for a little devotional?"

6. "Hi, angel!"

5. "Don't worry. I'm attracted to you purely in a spiritual way."

4. "I'm Episcopalian. What's your sign?"

3. "I think you're sitting on my Bible."

2. "Read any good Bible passages lately?"

1. "So, worship here often?"

—VIA DAVID BRIGGS, AP RELIGION WRITER

Pastor Denny J. Brake of Raleigh, North Carolina, observes that the reasons people give for not going to church also may be used as reasons for not going to bars.

"I stopped going to bars because…

- "Every time I went there they asked for money."
- "The bartender was the only one who spoke to me."
- "Some of the people who go there are hypocrites."
- "They don't sing the kind of songs I like."
- "My dad made me go with him when I was a kid."
- "You don't have to go to bars to be inebriated."

Bruce Burnside of Rockville, Maryland, passed on this limerick which he found in a 1974 bulletin of St. John's Episcopal Church, Georgetown, in Washington, DC:

> A meticulous postman named Hale
> Swam into the mouth of a whale.
>   He looked all about,
>   Crying, "Jonah, come out!
> Two cents' postage is due on your mail!"

"One Sunday when the lights went out before the late service at St. Peter's Episcopal Church, Ladue, Missouri, the rector's sermon was still in the computer, unable to be printed because of the power outage. When informed of this, the congregation applauded."

—*THE ANGLICAN DIGEST*

40 years of ministry prepared Pastor Lou for his retirement years.

© Steve Phelps

In Ireland, a young farmer named Mike wanted to get married, and he and his Maggie went to the priest to arrange for the wedding. The priest prepared them with all the instructions and then said: "Now, Mike, do you want the new rite or the old rite?"

"Aw, let's have the new rite," Mike said.

After dressing up in his best suit on the morning of the wedding, Mike remembered that he had to feed the cows, so he rolled up his pants legs and went into the barn. Then he went to church, but forgot to roll down his pants legs.

As he began the ceremony, the priest whispered to Mike: "Mike, pants down, pants down."

Mike looked at him and said: "Father, can't we have the old rite?"

—Archbishop John L. May of St. Louis

"A good sermon should have a good beginning and a good ending, and they should be as close together as possible."

—GEORGE BURNS

Some go to church to weep,
　　while others go to sleep.
Some go to tell their woes,
　　others to show their clothes.
Some go to hear the preacher,
　　others like the solo screecher.
Boys go to reconnoiter,
　　girls go because they orter.
Many go for good reflections,
　　precious few to help collections.

—JOE MAHER, OXNARD, CALIFORNIA

"I can't help it; I just love watching him cook his own dinner."

A Lutheran pastor who served a deaf congregation fumbled through his sermons weekly. Although he had a good background in sign language, the pastor didn't know the sign for "testament." So every time he referred to a Scripture verse, he had to spell out the word *Old* or *New* and then the word *Testament*.

One Sunday morning the pastor got creative and invented a sign for the missing word. When he read from the Psalms, he signed "Old" and then made the sign for the letter *T*. The congregation giggled. Then, when he read from Luke, he signed "New" and did the same *T* sign. Again, the congregation giggled.

After the service, some of the parishioners were still giggling as they greeted the pastor. Finally, a member told him: "Do you know what you read today? You read lessons from the old and new toilet."

—FMC MEMBER RONALD LEESE,
SPRING GROVE, PENNSYLVANIA

High-Tech Psalm

"The Lord is my programmer. I shall not crash. He installed His software on the hard disk of my heart; all of His commands are user-friendly; His directory guides me to the right choices for His name's sake. Even though I scroll through the problems of life, I will fear no bugs, for He is my backup; His password protects me; He prepares a menu before me in the presence of my enemies; His help is only a keystroke away. Surely goodness and mercy will follow me all the days of my life, and my file will be merged with His and saved forever."

—Author Unknown
via George Goldtrap, Ormond-by-the-Sea, Florida

A zealous, newly ordained minister was assigned to a small, rural parish. In his first sermon he condemned horse racing, and the sermon went over poorly. A deacon cautioned: "You should never preach against horse racing because this whole area is known for its fine horses. Many members of this congregation make their living off horses."

The next week the new pastor came down hard on the evils of smoking. Again his sermon fell flat. Many of his members grew tobacco.

On the third Sunday the preacher condemned whiskey drinking, only to discover that there was a big distillery less than five miles from the church.

The perplexed preacher called a board meeting and cried out: "What can I preach about?"

The answer came immediately from a woman in back: "Preach against them evil cannibals. There ain't one of them within two thousand miles of here."

—Rev. Dennis R. Fakes

"If you wish to get back to me during the day, my fax number is 426-8433 and my e-mail is bixby@bus.com."

A woman approached the clerk in a hardware store and ordered a box of spiders and a box of cockroaches. When the clerk asked why she wanted them, the woman answered: "I am the pastor's wife from the church down the street. Last night they voted my husband out of the church, and they told us to leave the parsonage *exactly* as we found it."

—REV. JAMES R. SWANSON

Forgive, O Lord
My little jokes on Thee,
And I'll forgive
Thy great big one on me.

—ROBERT FROST

HONK IF YOU LOVE JESUS!

A new teacher who is a devout Christian has a bumper sticker that says, "Honk if You Love Jesus!" She was driving home one day when she stopped at an intersection for a red traffic light.

While she was waiting, she closed her eyes and said a prayer thanking God for all His blessings. The car directly behind her started to honk.

Still in prayer, the woman said to herself, *Isn't it nice that he loves Jesus!* Then several more cars started to honk, too. *What a great witness—all these Christians behind me!* she thought.

She looked in her rearview mirror, and saw the man in the car behind her getting out of his car. "He probably wants to share his faith with me," she said to herself.

Then she noticed that the light was green, so she stepped on the gas and drove through the intersection just before the light turned red.

In the rearview mirror, she saw the assembled faithful she had left behind. "The man who was in the car behind me was waving enthusiastically," she excitedly told her husband when she got home. "And all the other people who had been honking had opened their windows and also were waving enthusiastically. Some were giving the Hawaiian good-luck sign. My students told me it was the Hawaiian good-luck sign."

—VIA DR. JOHN A. DALLES
WEKIVA PRESBYTERIAN CHURCH, LONGWOOD, FLORIDA

"Preach the Gospel at all times. If necessary, use words."

—ST. FRANCIS OF ASSISI

Pastor Fred Anson of Gloria Dei Lutheran Church in Toledo, Ohio, knows from experience that the water in the baptismal font can be too cold or too hot.

At his former church, during the rite of baptism, he reached into the baptismal font and discovered that the water was ice-cold. When he placed the water on the baby's head, the baby, he said, "let out a yell that would have raised Lazarus from the tomb."

When he came to Gloria Dei Lutheran Church, he made sure to ask the ushers to put warm water in the baptismal font. The usher followed instructions and put the lid on the font.

When the time came to baptize a baby during the worship service, the parents and sponsors were standing around the font. When Pastor Anson removed the lid, a cloud of steam rose from the baptismal font.

"I will never forget the look on the mother's face,"

says Anson. "I motioned for the usher and whispered to him to bring some cold water and put it into the font. The baptism then proceeded. After the service, I told the mother, 'My intention was to baptize your baby, not parboil it.'"

"All the members of my church tithe," one pastor told another pastor. "They all give ten percent of what they ought to be giving."

—VIA BRUCE H. BURNSIDE, ROCKVILLE, MARYLAND

Question: "What do you get if you cross a praying mantis with a termite?"
Answer: "An insect that says grace before he eats your house."

After the birth of their child, an Episcopal priest, wearing his clerical collar, visited his wife in the hospital. He greeted her with a hug and a kiss, and he gave her another hug and a kiss when he left.

Later, the wife's roommate commented: "Gee, your pastor is sure friendlier than mine."

On his very first day in office, a new pastor got a call from his predecessor. He congratulated him on his new charge and told him that in the center drawer of his desk he had left three envelopes, all numbered, which he was to open in order when he got into trouble.

After a short-lived honeymoon with the congregation, the heat began to rise and the minister decided to open the first envelope. His predecessor advised him:

"Blame me for the problem. After all, I'm long gone and have problems of my own; and if it will help, point out my shortcomings as the reason things are bad."

That worked for awhile, but then things got sour again. The pastor opened the second envelope, which read: "Blame the denomination. They're big and rich. They can take it."

That worked well for awhile, but then the storm clouds gathered again. In desperation the pastor went to the drawer and opened the third envelope. It said: "Prepare three envelopes."

—REV. RONALD H. WEINELT OF MCDONOUGH, GEORGIA
FOUNDER OF THE ASSOCIATION OF BATTERED CLERGY

"Few sinners are saved after the first twenty minutes of a sermon."

—MARK TWAIN

A young preacher had been called to a small rural church and appeared for his first sermon on Sunday morning. To his dismay he found that one of the parishioners had brought his dog to the service. He spoke politely to the dog's owner and asked if he would kindly remove the animal. The man obligingly took the dog out, then returned to his seat.

After the service, the church deacons rebuked the new preacher for insulting one of their staunch members. They pointed out that the dog made no trouble; he had been accompanying his master to church for years.

That afternoon the young preacher called at the home of the dog's owner and apologized.

"Don't worry a bit about it, Reverend," the man replied. "It all worked out. I wouldn't have had my dog hear that sermon for anything in the world."

—SHERWOOD ELIOT WIRT, AUTHOR, *JESUS: MAN OF JOY*

"Just where have you been for the last three days?"

Frowning is hard work: It takes forty-three muscles to frown but only seventeen muscles to smile.

If the U.S. government were in place when God talked to Moses, the conversation might have gone something like this:

God said, "Moses, I have some good news and some bad news for you. The good news is that you are going to lead My people Israel out of Egypt, and you are going to have to part the Red Sea to do it."

"And the bad news?" Moses asked.

"You have to fill out all the environmental impact forms before leaving."

—VIA DONALD L. COOPER, M.D., STILLWATER, OKLAHOMA

"The worst thing about being married to a prophet besides washing his sackcloth is the fact that you can never throw him a surprise party."

© Dik LaPine

"Live so that you wouldn't be ashamed to sell the family parrot to the town gossip."

—WILL ROGERS

"We carry our religion as if it were a headache. There is neither joy nor power nor inspiration in it, none of the grandeur of the unsearchable riches of Christ about it, none of the passion of hilarious confidence in God."

—OSWALD CHAMBERS
VIA GEORGE METTAM, WHEAT RIDGE, COLORADO

"After a very delicious fried chicken dinner prepared by the Swedish Lutheran ladies at a missionary society conference held in our small church, the conversation moved from the dinner to other small talk. The speaker for the conference asked my mother, a pastor's wife: 'How many children do you have?'

"In the noise and commotion, my mother thought he asked, 'How many chickens do you have?'—a common question because most families in our small community had chickens in their backyards.

"My mother replied: 'I really don't know because my husband takes care of them. They stay penned up in the backyard, and he sees to it that meal scraps get out to them. Every now and then, one gets out, but that doesn't happen very often.'"

—ALBERT O. KARLSTROM, CHAMPAIGN, ILLINOIS

The pope went to New York City and hailed a cab from the airport to St. Patrick's Church. Because he was running late, the pope asked the cabby to speed it up, but the cabby refused. Finally, the frustrated pope demanded that the cabby pull over and let him drive.

As soon as the cabby gave in to the pope's wish, a policeman stopped them. When the officer looked inside the cab, his eyes widened, and he ran back to his car to call the police chief.

"I've stopped a speeding cab, but there's someone very important inside," he told the chief. "What do I do?"

"Give the driver a ticket," the chief growled.

"But he's got a very important passenger."

"Well, who is it?" the chief asked. "The mayor? The governor? The president?"

"I don't know," the officer replied. "But the pope is driving him."

—Mrs. Harriet Adams, Morton, Pennsylvania

Episcopal Aerobics Rite II

Stand	Sit or Stand
Sit	Stand or Kneel
Stand	Walk
Sit	Sit, Stand, or Kneel
Stand	Stand
Sit Still	Kneel
Stand	Stand
Kneel	Walk
Stand and Hug	Shake (hands)

—Church of the Redeemer, Midlothian, Virginia
The Anglican Digest

For those who are to preach, it is customary in my country that the preacher kneels for prayer before entering the pulpit. The daughter of one of my clergy noticed her father praying Sunday after Sunday as he prepared to mount the pulpit. She asked her daddy what he prayed for. The priest replied that he was asking God to help him preach a better sermon, whereupon the child asked, "Well, why doesn't He?"

—ARCHBISHOP DESMOND TUTU OF SOUTH AFRICA

"George Washington, as a boy, was ignorant of the commonest accomplishments of youth; he could not even lie."

—MARK TWAIN

"Be of good cheer; I have overcome the world."

—JOHN 16:33 (NASB)

© Steve Phelps

It was a very hot day, and the air conditioner at Christ Episcopal Church in Rockville, Maryland, had failed. The pastor, Rev. Linda Poindexter, walked to the pulpit, looked out at the sweltering congregation, and gave this ten-word sermon: "Hot, isn't it? Hell's like that. Don't go there! Amen."

—VIA BRUCE H. BURNSIDE, ROCKVILLE, MARYLAND

When a pastor joined a local service club in his community, some of the members of his congregation made up the nametags for the group. They decided to play a practical joke on the pastor by labeling his occupation as "Hog Caller" on his nametag.

When the pastor saw his nametag, he commented: "They usually call me the 'Shepherd of the Sheep,' but I suppose our members know themselves better than I do."

—VIA REV. DENNIS FAKES, LINDSBORG, KANSAS

The inevitable finally occurred—a potluck with nothing but baked beans.

Lawrence W. Althouse, a retired United Methodist pastor in Dallas who writes a syndicated newspaper column, tells this story:

"Many years ago, when I was working in a suburban New York church, I was asked to take part in an ecumenical Easter dawn pageant held at the Bronx River Parkway. At 5:15 A.M. I was zipping down the parkway. But within moments, the flashing red lights of a police car pulled me over.

"I was in the costume of an angel—complete with wings and halo. When the officer walked toward me and looked in the window, I thought his eyes were going to pop out of his head.

"He regained his composure and asked, 'Do you have any idea how fast you were going?'

"I told him I didn't, but I really had to hurry because 'I've got to get to the Resurrection on time.'

"The officer stared at me, his face clouded over, and he blurted out: 'Go! Just go!' And I did."

—FROM "THE BIBLE SPEAKS," COMMUNITY PRESS SERVICE
FRANKFORT, KENTUCKY

"It is requisite for the relaxation of the mind that we make use, from time to time, of playful deeds and jokes…"

—THOMAS AQUINAS, *SUMMA THEOLOGICA*

"Two quick ways to disaster: (1) Take nobody's advice. (2) Take everybody's advice."

—RALPH CANSLER, COHUTTA, GEORGIA

NOAH'S MIDLIFE CRISIS

Tommy DiNardo of Virginia Beach, Virginia, is an engineer-turned-comedian-turned-engineer. The following reflections on Noah are from his audiocassette The Best of Tommy DiNardo:

"I'd like to live as long as Noah lived. Noah lived for 950 years. He built an ark, but it took him a hundred years. Apparently, it was a government contract.

"Nine-hundred-and-fifty years old! How does that work? Do you look like you're 100 years old for 850 years? Or do you look like you're 50 at 500?

"Do you go through a series of midlife crises or just the big one at 400? You know, wearing the gold chains and driving a sports chariot.

"Can you imagine Noah at 400 having a midlife crisis discussion with his wife? 'You know, honey,' he says, 'I just want to do something different with my life. I want to make an impact.'

"His wife says, 'Well, honey, you talk to God!'

" 'Yeah, but so does Pat Robertson. I need something really different.'

" 'Well, you can always finish that boat you've been diddling with…'

" 'Get off my back!'

"What do you say to someone who is 950 years old? 'Noah, you look great! You don't look a day over 800, man! It's that fat-free diet, isn't it?'

"What do you say at the guy's funeral? *'Finally!'*?

"The Bible tells you everything, but it tells you nothing about what Noah did before he was a carpenter. I did a little research, and I found out that before Noah was a carpenter, he sold Amway.

"Noah was a heck of an engineer—that's for sure—building that huge boat. I was an engineer before I went into comedy. I switched when NASA built the Hubble telescope. Two billion dollars for fuzzy pictures of Pluto! Yeah, that engineer was a comedian too."

"Every evening I turn my troubles over to God—He's going to be up all night anyway."

—DONALD J. MORGAN, COLUMBUS, OHIO

After the church service, a pastor told a woman, "I noticed your husband walked out in the middle of my sermon. I hope I didn't say something that offended him."

"Not at all," replied the wife. "My husband has been walking in his sleep for years."

"Sir, would you come with me? It has come to our attention you have been peeking when the pastor says, "With every head bowed, every eye closed..."

REPORT OF THE SEARCH COMMITTEE

We have investigated a number of candidates for the ministry, but we regret to report that none seems suitable. Here are the comments on those that we have considered so far:

Noah: Has 120 years of preaching experience but not a single convert.

Moses: Stutters. Also loses his temper.

Abraham: Goes to Egypt in hard times. Sometimes lies when in trouble.

David: Likes the ladies. Might be considered for minister of music if he had not fallen.

Solomon: A reputation for wisdom, but does not always practice what he preaches.

Elijah: Inconsistent. Folds under pressure. Retreats into caves.

Isaiah: Has unclean lips; admitted it in a worship service.

Jeremiah: Too emotional. Cries a lot. Alarmist. "Pain in the neck," some say.

Amos: No seminary training. Should stick to picking figs.

John the Baptist: Popular, but lacks tact and dresses like a hippie. (Considering his diet, he would not be happy at church suppers.)

Peter: Actually denied he knew Christ. Could not lead evangelism committee.

Paul: Preaches well, but shabby appearance. Long sermons; people sleep.

Timothy: Has potential. Background questionable. Too young.

Jesus: Offends large segments of the audience when He preaches. Very controversial. He even offended the search committee.

Judas: Practical. Leadership abilities. Served on an executive committee. Good with money. Conservative spender. Cares for the poor. We were ready to make him our choice when he hung himself.

—ADAPTED WITH PERMISSION OF *THE ANGLICAN DIGEST*

"Preparing for a sermon, our pastor, John Koch, of Trinity Assembly of God in Crivitz, Wisconsin, got a great idea. On Saturday night, Pastor Koch and a few congregation members trashed the sanctuary with garbage, pop bottles and cans, old clothes and shoes, newspapers, and even socks hanging from the chandeliers. It was a mess!

"Later that evening, a local police officer was checking the area and noticed the side door was unlocked. He walked in with his flashlight and, to his surprise, saw the mess. He got on his radio and told the dispatcher to call the pastor. The dispatcher called the youth pastor, Jay Fisher, and told him, 'Your church has been broken into and ransacked.'

"'No, it's supposed to be that way,' Pastor Jay replied, explaining that it was part of the object lesson for the next day's service.

"The next day, people hesitated to even set foot in the sanctuary. Others ran wild. Pastor Koch started leading songs and then said, 'Let's clean up this mess.'

"In five minutes, with the help of the entire congregation, the sanctuary was clean. Pastor Koch then began his sermon and preached about getting the sin out of our lives so that we could be able to really come to God and worship Him."

—MARK AND SUSAN BRADBURY, WAUSAUKEE, WISCONSIN

"I'm leaving the church and taking my favorite pew with me!"

© Jonny Hawkins

Question: How many bass-baritones from a church choir does it take to change a light bulb?

Answer: Three. One to climb the ladder and do the job, and the other two to sit there and say, "Isn't that a little too high for you?"

—BRUCE H. BURNSIDE, ROCKVILLE, MARYLAND

A group of women were talking together. One woman said, "Our congregation is sometimes down to thirty or forty on a Sunday."

Another said: "That's nothing. Sometimes our congregation is down to six or seven."

A maiden lady in her seventies added her bit, "Why, it's so bad in our church on Sundays that when the minister says 'dearly beloved,' it makes me blush."

—REV. CLIFFORD WAITE, OAKWOOD, ONTARIO

Two bees met near a flowering bush. "How was your summer?" one bee asked.

"Too cold. Too much rain. Not enough flowers or pollen," the second bee replied.

"There's a bar mitzvah going on down the block. Lots of flowers and fruit. Why don't you go down there?" the first bee suggested.

"Thanks!" the second bee said and flew away.

Later, the two bees encountered each other again. "How was the bar mitzvah?" asked the first bee.

"Wonderful!" said the other bee.

"But what's that on your head?" the first bee asked.

"A yarmulke," the second bee answered. "I didn't want them to think I was a WASP."

—VIA SARA A. FORTENBERRY, HERMITAGE, TENNESSEE

After he moved from a church in Connecticut to become rector at St. Ambrose Episcopal Church in Boulder, Colorado, Fellowship of Merry Christians member Rev. John Elledge commented: "The people in my town in Connecticut seemed to think that one of the gifts of the Spirit is suspicion."

When he entered the pulpit, the preacher realized that he had forgotten his sermon notes. He immediately apologized: "Since I forgot my sermon notes, I must rely on the Lord for this sermon. I promise to come better prepared next Sunday."

—REV. DENNIS R. FAKES, LINDSBORG, KANSAS

YOU MIGHT BE IN A COUNTRY CHURCH IF ...

Lutheran Pastor Ron Birk of San Marcos, Texas, is a humorist and Texas goat rancher whose ancestors were involved in farming and ranching. The following is reprinted with permission from his book *You Might Be in a Country Church If...* (LangMarc Publishing, San Antonio, Texas):

You might be in a country church if...

- The doors are never locked.
- The call to worship is "Y'all come on in!"
- People grumble about Noah letting coyotes on the ark.
- The preacher says, "I'd like to ask Bubba to help take up the offering"—and five guys stand up.
- The restroom is outside.

- Opening day of deer hunting season is recognized as an official church holiday.
- A member requests to be buried in his four-wheel-drive truck because "I ain't never been in a hole it couldn't get me out of."
- Never in its entire one-hundred-year history has one of its pastors had to buy any meat or vegetables.
- When it rains, everybody's smiling.
- Prayers regarding the weather are a standard part of every worship service.
- A singing group is known as "The O.K. Chorale."
- The church directory doesn't have last names.
- The pastor wears boots.
- The only time people lock their cars in the parking lot is during the summer—and then only so their neighbors can't leave them a bag of squash.

- Four generations of one family sit together in worship every Sunday.
- Baptism is referred to as "branding."
- Finding and returning lost sheep is not just a parable.
- You miss worship one Sunday morning and by two o'clock that afternoon you have had a dozen phone calls inquiring about your health.
- High notes on the organ set dogs in the parking lot to howling.
- People wonder when Jesus fed the five thousand whether the two fish were bass or catfish.
- People think "Rapture" is what happens when you lift something too heavy.
- The cemetery is on such barren ground that people are buried with a sack of fertilizer to help them rise on Judgment Day.

- There is no such thing as a "secret" sin.
- It's not heaven, but you can see heaven from there.
- The final words of the benediction are "Y'all come on back now, ya hear!"

© Jonny Hawkins

Quaker humorist Tom Mullen was visiting his brother Frank, who lives in New York. Frank told Tom that New York City has the biggest and longest garbage strikes in the country, and the garbage piles up on the streets.

Frank said that when a garbage strike was called before Christmas one year, he solved the problem by wrapping his garbage daily as if it were a Christmas gift and putting it in the backseat of his car, leaving the car door unlocked. Invariably a thief would steal the package.

"For health and the constant enjoyment of life, give me a keen and ever-present sense of humor; it is the next best thing to an abiding faith in Providence."

—GEORGE B. CHEEVER

"According to my horoscope, this is a good week to preach against false doctrines."

© Jonny Hawkins

PRAYER OF A MELLOWING NUN

The Joyful Noiseletter consulting editor Barbara Shlemon Ryan of Brea, California, invited readers to reflect on this whimsical prayer of an anonymous seventeenth-century nun:

"Lord, Thou knowest better than I know myself that I am growing older and will someday be old. Keep me from the fatal habit of thinking I must say something on every subject and on every occasion. Release me from craving to straighten out everybody's affairs. Make me thoughtful but not moody; helpful but not bossy. With my vast store of wisdom it seems a pity not to use it all, but Thou knowest that I want a few friends at the end.

"Keep my mind free from the recital of endless details; give me wings to get to the point. Seal my lips on my aches and pains. They are increasing, and love of rehearsing them is becoming sweeter as the years go by.

"I dare not ask for grace enough to enjoy the tales of others' pains, but help me to endure them with patience. I dare not ask for an improved memory, but for a growing humility and a lessening cocksureness when my memory seems to clash with the memories of others.

"Teach me the glorious lesson that occasionally I may be mistaken.

"Keep me reasonably sweet; I do not want to be a saint. Some of them are so hard to live with—but a sour old person is one of the crowning works of the devil. Give me the ability to see good things in unexpected places and talents in unexpected people. And, give me, O Lord, the grace to tell them so."

⟲

A man took a fancy to a church notorious for its exclusiveness. He told the minister he wished to join. The minister sought to evade the issue by suggesting that the man reflect more carefully on the matter and pray for guidance.

The following day, the man told the minister: "I prayed, sir, and the Lord asked me what church I wanted to join. When I told Him it was yours, He laughed and said, 'You can't get in there. I've been trying to get in that church for ten years myself, and *I* can't get in.'"

The telephone number of the rectory of Whitesand Parish in Kamsack, Saskatchewan, is listed in the white pages of the telephone book as "Anglican Rectory." When the rector, Rev. Ian C. Payne, answered the phone recently, a telemarketing caller asked, "Is Mr. Anglican home, please?"

"Welcome to *Fantasy Island*, Youth Pastor Dave! Your fantasy of living your life without any teenager, parent, or senior pastor has been arranged."

© Dik LaPine

C. Justin Clements, director of the Office of Stewardship and Development in the Catholic Diocese of Evansville, Indiana, went through one of his parish hymnals and put together the following "Hymn Game," assigning hymns to various professions and people.

"All Are Welcome"—The Motel Manager's Hymn

"All Good Gifts"—The Lobbyist's Hymn

"All Shall Be Well"—The Hospital Administrator's Hymn

"All That Is Hidden"—The Magician's Hymn

"All That We Have"—The Taxpayer's Hymn

"Behold the Wood"—The Carpenter's Hymn

"Change Our Hearts"—The Heart Surgeon's Hymn

"Come Away to the Skies"—The NASA Hymn

"Come to Me, O Weary Traveler"—The Motel 6 Hymn

"Come to Set Us Free"—The Bail Bondsman's Hymn

"Come to the House"—The Realtor's Hymn

"Come to the Water"—The Lifeguard's Hymn

"Comfort My People"—The Masseuse's Hymn

"Create a Clean Heart" —The Angioplasty Hymn

"Eye Has Not Seen" —The Optometrist's Hymn

"For the Healing"—The HMO Accountant's Hymn

"Gather Us Together"—The Board Chairman's Hymn

"How Firm a Foundation"—The Contractor's Hymn

"How Great Thou Art"—The Weight Watcher's Hymn

"How Lovely Is Your Dwelling Place"—The Interior
   Decorator's Hymn

"I Saw Water Flowing"—The Plumber's Hymn

"I Want to Call You"—The Long-Distance Telephone
   Company Hymn

"Lord, You Give the Great Commission"—The Sales-
   person's Hymn

"Out of Darkness"—The Electrician's Hymn

"Shall We Gather at the River"—The Fisherman's Hymn

"Somebody's Knockin' at Your Door"—The Jeho-
vah's Witnesses' Hymn

"Walk in the Reign"—Gene Kelly's Hymn

"We Shall Rise Again"—The Baker's Hymn

"What Star Is This?"—The Astronomer's Hymn

"Give me, Lord, a soul that knows nothing of
boredom, groans, and sighs. Never let me be
overly concerned for this inconstant thing I call
me. Lord, give me a sense of humor so that I
may take some happiness from this life and
share it with others."

—SIR THOMAS MORE (1478–1535)

"Brother Helvey is here with the black box from last night's sermon to see if we can find out what went wrong."

THE TOP TEN THINGS PEOPLE THINK ABOUT WHILE SINGING A HYMN

When he was pastor of Zion Lutheran Church in Doylestown, Ohio, Rev. Paul Lintern started a comedy club called "Saturday Night Alive" in his church social hall. A parishioner played music on an electronic keyboard. A troupe of singers led the audience in a variety of songs. Actors put on skits. And Lintern warmed up the audience with jokes—for instance, this take-off on David Letterman's "Top Ten List"

10. The pot roast.

9. What does the pastor wear under robes?

8. Will the person behind me ever hit the right note?

7. Ninety minutes till kickoff.

6. Did I turn off the curling iron?

5. The likelihood of the ceiling fan falling and hitting me on the head.

4. How many people have lost more hair than I have?

3. How would the hymn sound if Metallica played it?

2. Are there doughnuts at fellowship?

1. How many more verses?

"Our Presbyterian church once had an interim minister who, unnerved by the size of our congregation, made a couple of very funny bloopers during her sermons. She referred to Paul's letter to the 'Philippines.' And at Christmas she raised her arms to heaven and declared, 'Today, Christ is bored.'"

—LORRAINE AHO, NOVATO, CALIFORNIA

Chronicling the story of a rebuilding project at First Congregational Church, Murphys, California, the building committee chair reported to the congregation:

"It was discovered during the building program that the left side of the ninety-year-old sanctuary actually extends five feet into the street. That means that those of you sitting on the left side of the building are actually sitting in the street. We have discovered a unique ministry here in Murphys. We have found out how to minister to street people without even leaving the church building."

—REV. JANE GIBBONS HUANG
FIRST CONGREGATIONAL CHURCH, MURPHYS, CALIFORNIA

An egotist is someone who is always me-deep in conversation.

—GEORGE GOLDTRAP, ORMOND-BY-THE-SEA, FLORIDA

"Here I am, Lord. A New Year. A fresh awakening. Ready to serve You with all my strength. Ready to wrestle with Satan. Ready to serve others and fight for right. Ready to win the lottery…"

© Ed Sullivan

FMC member Pastor Joseph LoMusio of Temple Baptist Church, Fullerton, California, the author of *If I Should Die Before I Live*, says he heard of a mortuary director who signs all his correspondence "Eventually Yours."

TOP TEN EXCUSES FOR NOT ATTENDING CHURCH

Sorry I missed church, but...

10. I can find God in nature.
9. I prefer watching televangelists. (There's just something about a remote control that makes me feel like I'm in control of my own spiritual life.)
8. It would make me miss my Zen class.
7. There are too many hypocrites in church. Besides, it interferes with my tee-time.

6. There's too much hugging and real warmth.

5. There isn't enough hugging and real warmth.

4. I went once, but I didn't recognize the place without the lilies or poinsettias.

3. I'm an atheist—I swear!

2. Even Jesus wouldn't have gone if He'd had to wear pantyhose.

1. The dog ate my offering.

> —*THE DISCIPLE*
> REPRINTED WITH PERMISSION OF CHRISTIAN BOARD OF
> PUBLICATION, ST. LOUIS, MISSOURI, © 1998

Question: What do you call the people who regularly evacuate the rear pew at the sound of the first note of the recessional hymn and well before the priest exits?

Answer: The faithful departed.

> —FR. RAYMOND G. HEISEL
> CHURCH OF THE EPIPHANY/CHURCH OF ST. ROSE,
> SODUS, NEW YORK

"I thought sure this would be the Lent
when his long-dormant spiritual values
would come to the fore."

BIBLIMERICKS

The confusion of language at Babel
did not put a stop to the gabble;
   For folks north and south
   Still ran off at the mouth;
But it messed up a good game of Scrabble.

The Pharoah encouraged his daughter
To bathe as a good princess oughter;
   But he wasn't too glad
   When she hollered, "Hey, Dad!
Just look what I found in the water!"

—LOIS BLANCHARD EADES, DICKSON, TENNESSEE

"Don't let yesterday take up too much of today."

—WILL ROGERS

CHRISTMAS GIFTS FOR THE CLERGY

The catalog of Balmy Clergy Supply, Inc. offered the following special Christmas gift suggestions for clergy, according to The Joyful Noiseletter *consulting editor Rev. David R. Francoeur of Stuart, Florida:*

LAUGHING ALMS BASIN

In order to help your church members have a more cheerful attitude about giving, Balmy has developed the Laughing Alms Basin. At the touch of a hand, a small digitized recording of men and women laughing joyfully is projected from a speaker located on the bottom of the alms basin. Recent studies have shown that the regular use of this jovial soundtrack increases giving by 12–15 percent.

Order No. 965-G Laughing Alms Basin …$167.50 (batteries not included)

THE BALMY INVISIBLE PLATE VACUUM

Clergy have to attend many church meals and dinner parties in members' homes, and a significant number of clergy report they have difficulty keeping their weight down.

The Balmy Invisible Plate Vacuum consists of a small but powerful pump linked to a five-mil plastic bag, strapped to the pastor's back, with a long hose designed to run down the sleeve of a jacket or long-sleeve shirt. After eating a modest amount, the pastor places the end of the sleeve an inch above the plate, the vacuum pump is activated, and the contents of the plate are quickly sucked into the plastic bag. With its small size and ultra-quiet motor, the Balmy Invisible Plate Vacuum is the perfect gift for weight-conscious clergy.

Order No. 872-E Invisible Plate Vacuum…$521.32 (includes 50 bags)

May the sun always shine
    on your windowpane.
May a rainbow be certain
    to follow each rain.
May the hand of a friend
    always be near you.
May God fill your heart
    with gladness to cheer you.

—OLD IRISH BLESSING

Rev. Paul J. Davis, editor of *The Desert Wind*, newsletter of St. Anthony on the Desert Episcopal Church, Scottsdale, Arizona, passes on the following item:

"Our Newcomer Committee spent part of their time at their last meeting spraying ants in West Hall. Fr. Hal Daniell began the meeting by saying, 'Let us spray.'"

"I'd like permission to play God with my staff for just a short time tomorrow."

© Steve Phelps

NOAH'S TOP TEN

10. Strange! We haven't seen another boat for weeks.

9. If only I'd brought along more rhino litter!

8. How many times around this place makes a mile?

7. I never want to sleep in a waterbed again.

6. I wonder what my friends are doing right now.

5. An outboard motor would have made this more exciting!

4. Fish for supper—again?

3. Does anyone have more Dramamine?

2. What? You don't have film to photograph the rainbow?

1. I should have killed those darn mosquitoes when I had the chance!

—PASTOR PAUL W. KUMMER
GRACE LUTHERAN CHURCH, DESTIN, FLORIDA

"Jewish spirituality has always found a place for humor. It has not forgotten that the biblical God is a God of unexpected turns, twists, and surprises. God plays; God teases! Jewish spirituality loves the humor of a laughing insight into religion. Even the classics—the Talmud, the Zohar, the Hasidic stories—revel in the humorous tidbit."

—MATTHIAS NEWMAN, OSB, *America*

"Christianity is the most humorous point of view in the history of the world."

—SOREN KIERKEGAARD

Rev. Ken Grambo of Camrose, Alberta, who serves two Lutheran congregations in Alberta, was calling attention to various parts of the service printed in the Sunday bulletin. "Let us join now in confessing our sins, which are printed in the bulletin," he said.

Entry in George Washington's diary:

"There being no Episcopal minister present in the place, I went to hear morning service performed in the Dutch Reformed Church—which, being in a language not a word of which I understood, I was in no danger of becoming a proselyte to its religion by the eloquence of the preacher."

"Many folks want to serve God, but only as advisers."

—SR. MONIQUE RYSAVY, OWATONNA, MINNESOTA

"The good Lord didn't create anything without a purpose, but the fly comes close."

—MARK TWAIN

Syndicated columnist James J. Kilpatrick, a well-known wordsmith, wrote a column about the art of overkill. "In our business, the writing business, sometimes we try too hard," Kilpatrick observed. "The novelist comes down with adjectivitis, the preacher succumbs to bloviation, and the newspaperman tries his hand at purple prose."

According to Webster's World Dictionary, the word "bloviation" does indeed exist. "To bloviate" is "to speak at some length bombastically or rhetorically."

The place to be happy is here;
The time to be happy is now;
The way to be happy is to make others so.

—VIA PASTOR JOHN J. WALKER
FIRST CHRISTIAN CHURCH, POST, TEXAS

"Humor is another of the soul's weapons in the fight for self-preservation."

—VICTOR FRANKL

David E. Sumner, a former editor of the newspaper of the Episcopal Diocese of Southern Ohio, shared the following ads which he once placed—tongue-in-cheek—in that newspaper.

IS YOUR CHURCH INSURED AGAINST ACTS OF GOD?

Do it now, while our special low, low premiums last. You never know who will be confirmed, ordained, or instituted there tomorrow. By next year, it could be too late. Contact our friendly agents by consulting your telephone directory.

Travelon Insurance
"We don't pray—we pay."

THE CHURCH IN THE WOODS

Thursdays—10:00 A.M.
Healing Service

"For all of those afflicted,
wounded, and distressed
by ecclesiastical politics."

"A vacation is when you pack seven suitcases, three small children, a mother-in-law, two dogs, and say: 'It's good to get away from it all.'"

—REV. JAMES A. SIMPSON

"He says that if we can distribute the food to the 5000, then He might let us cater a Promise Keeper's conference."

© Dik LaPine

"A clown is a poet in action. He can show us how to laugh at ourselves because his own laughter was born of tears. The clown has confronted sorrow and suffering and pain, and transformed them into compassion. Clowns are healers, and the world has never needed them more than it does now."

—Sr. Marie-Celeste Fadden, OCD
Clowns and Children of the World, Reno, Nevada

More Bloopers

James L. Sullivan recalled that, when he was president of a Baptist publishing house, the printing of a Sunday school lesson was halted when the title "Paul Pleads for a Slave" was printed as "Paul Pleads for a Shave."

"Harpeth Hills Church of Christ, 1949 Old Hickory Boulevard, Nashville, Tennessee, will present a series of community classes on various subjects throughout this month and into March. The classes offered include 'How to Lose 100 Pounds, from 7–9 P.M. Monday.'"

—GEORGE GOLDTRAP, ORMOND-BY-THE-SEA, FLORIDA

In a sermon at First United Methodist Church, the Reverend P. Thomas Wachterhauser observed: "Have you noticed the problem created for ministers by the large bulletin boards out in front of a church? The sermon title is placed just above the name of the preacher of the day. A year ago, the sign read: "Who Killed Jesus? Dr. Alfred T. Bamsey." Not long ago, the sign read: "Nothing to Wear. Rev. Marsha M. Woolley." This morning, the sign reads: "The Perfect Christian. Rev. P. Thomas Wachterhauser."

—WINSLOW FOX, M.D., ANN ARBOR, MICHIGAN